Workbook

Girl, Wash Your Face:

Stop Believing the Lies About Who You Are so You Can Become Who You Were Meant to Be

Rachel Hollis

Max Help Books

By Dan Young

Attention: Bonus Download

Thank you for your purchase of Max Help Workbooks

Get Free Workbooks with __Any Purchase__ of Max Help Workbooks

Every purchase comes with a FREE download!

Get it Now

or Click Here.

Table of Contents

How to Use This Workbook for Enhanced Application

Complete beginners can begin using this workbook for Girl, Wash Your Face: Stop Believing the Lies About Who You Are so You Can Become Who You Were Meant to Be by Rachel Hollis to get immediate help of the major lessons found in this book.

The goal of this workbook is to help even the newest readers to begin applying major lessons from Girl, Wash Your Face: Stop Believing the Lies About Who You Are so You Can Become Who You Were Meant to Be by Rachel Hollis Results have shown us that learning is retained better through repeated real-life applications.

By using this workbook, readers will find categorized lessons that we believed were major in defining the crucial messages of the author in the book. There are questions devoted both for self or corporate usage and actionable steps through charts and analysis tables to stimulate a contined engagement with the main lessons in the book.

Take out a pencil, pen, or whatever digital technology you would put to use to jot down, implement, and make happen. And don't forget to have fun - that'll also keep you *learning*.

The Background Story of Girl, Wash Your Face

Rachel Hollis is the founder and CEO of her own media company called Chic Media. From an incredibly early age, Hollis has proven her potential, as she was even recognized as one of the 30 most successful entrepreneurs under the age of 30 by INC Magazine. On her website, she has written articles in which she expresses her opinion and even personal anecdotes about everyday topics. Hollis has shown that what it takes to be successful is not a college degree or a lot of money, but to trust our dreams and let them guide us.

Hollis has said that, like when writing articles for her website, when she wrote *Girl, Wash Your F*ace, she often did so by addressing issues she had been thinking about or even working on in her own life. In our lives there can be problems of all kinds, whether they are internal problems like anxieties or anger, or external problems like problems in our relationship or work. Hollis uses those moments in which she tries to analyze the problem she is going through or one she has already gone through to be able to write in a more free and realistic way. This is because when she tries to decipher the origins of a problem, she has to look for its roots and unfold it, so when she describes it she does it in a more complete and personal way. Hollis said that she does not think about what she is going to write beforehand, but rather uses moments like these in which the feelings or thoughts are fresh to express them through writing and thus be able to share them with us.

She said in an interview that the reason she wanted to write *Girl, Wash Your Face* was because she wanted to help all the women who might be facing situations like the ones she had faced. She wanted to make them understand that they have the true power of their lives to fulfill their dreams and overcome the obstacles that may arise. In addition, she said that she included many anecdotes and personal experiences to show readers that she has also gone through many of the things that they may be going through and that she managed to get ahead despite the obstacles. Hollis provides important suggestions and tips that she has learned from her own experiences and hardships.

Executive Summary of Girl, Wash Your Face: Stop Believing the Lies About Who You Are so You Can Become Who You Were Meant to Be

Girl, Wash Your Face is a book written by TheChicSite.com founder, Rachel Hollis. She is also the founder and CEO of Chic Media, her own media company. Through her business, Hollis has made contracts with renowned companies such as JCPenney, Target, Walmart, among others. On the other side, Hollis dedicates her website to discussing lifestyle issues. In the same way and with the same energy, Hollis, through her book, shares with readers many of the problems she has had to overcome in her life and what she has done to overcome them, so this book is of great help to all women who want to know more about how to approach their problems correctly and how to learn from them in such a way that they can improve their lives more each and every day.

Hollis uses the titles of each chapter of *Girl, Wash Your Face* to reveal a specific lie she has told herself at some point in her life. These lies had usually gone unnoticed, making her feel undervalued, overwhelmed, or eager to give up everything she had fought for. She relates not only her anecdotes regarding these lies, but also describes the misfortunes they brought to her life by not knowing how to recognize them more quickly. However, that is not all. Hollis also includes many tips and suggestions that any woman can follow in order to overcome problems similar to those she has overcome.

One of the topics that Hollis addresses most is taking control of our own lives so that we can overcome obstacles and follow our dreams. This is especially important, because through our dreams is revealed the path we must follow in order to have the life we have always wanted. Hollis motivates readers to gather courage and get ahead of any difficulties they may encounter, because although problems are inevitable, our actions are what define the real outcomes of these problems. The author says that we must all be our own boss, our own hero.

Hollis affirms that wanting to seek happiness does not make us selfish nor does it distance us from our religion. In the same way, to be happy we don't have to believe in someone or something greater and more important than ourselves. We must be aware that only we have the power to turn our lives into what we want, to live as we wish, to be happy as we always wanted to be. She emphasizes that there are things that are beyond our control, but that does not make them insurmountable, so we must fight, overcome those things, learn from them, and ultimately move on.

The author, on the other hand, explains how she has managed to achieve the success she has achieved— and still continues to achieve. The key to success is not in the money or career we have, but in our desire to follow our dreams, and our willingness to let ourselves be guided by them.

However, Hollis also says that we should not be too much driven by work, so we must maintain a balance between our life and our work.

Hollis is a person who has developed her full potential. However, she not only shares her experiences of success with us, but also shares the difficulties she has had in obtaining it and in her life in general. The author approaches issues and problems in a very impressive way, because besides allowing us to know her own experiences—both good and bad—in order to identify with her, she also makes us realize that many of the problems we may be facing are problems that we have the power to solve, the power to overcome. *Girl, Wash Your Face* is not only a self-help book, it is an invaluable guide that helps us realize that we can do it, that we can live our lives the way we want, that we can fulfill our dreams, and that nothing is impossible.

Lesson #1

Lesson #1: Focus on being the hero of your own life.

The Lesson Explained

Life can be so different. It can be enjoyable, fun, pleasant, while on the other hand, it can be sad, hard, painful, becoming a continuous suffering rather than a joy. However, how we approach every aspect of our own lives will determine greatly what it will be like later on. Our lives pass us by and give us opportunities that we have the choice to exploit or waste. When we use opportunities, our life improves, our perspective towards it changes and becomes more optimistic, so we can see more possibilities to be more productive, happy, and self-realized. Other times, we miss opportunities for one reason or another. The consequences of what may happen by missing an opportunity can vary greatly, especially because of the attitude the person takes after missing an opportunity.

The author states that we have control over our own lives, and therefore it is ourselves who lead it and our actions that shape it. We choose how to enjoy happy moments, how to exploit all the benefits or advantages that we have. On the other hand, we also choose how to face the problems and obstacles that our life may have, because even though they affect us or hinder our path, we can overcome them and shape our own destiny.

Hollis thinks we should be the heroes of our own lives. We must find the best way to live our lives and make ourselves happy. For many people, wanting to be happy is an act of selfishness or lack of faith, since seeking happiness depends on us. However, the author emphasizes that this is a lie that these people tell themselves. Seeking happiness for our own lives has nothing to do with being selfish or putting aside our faith. Besides, we don't have to believe in anything or anyone greater than ourselves. What we must do is to take control of our own lives and make the best of it. Therefore, if we are unhappy with our lives, it is something that only we ourselves can and must solve.

Application Exercise

To be the hero of your own life, you must manage it and decide what is best for you. Self-evaluate on a scale of 1 to 10 to determine how much you control your life.

1. There can be many problems that may arise. I always try to solve them my way. (10 = Always; 1 = Never)

1 2 3 4 5 6 7 8 9 10

2. Opportunities come and go. I'm always looking to use every one of these opportunities. (10 = Always; 1 = Never)

1 2 3 4 5 6 7 8 9 10

3. There are many kinds of jobs. I choose the one I like best. (10 = Always; 1 = Never)

1 2 3 4 5 6 7 8 9 10

4. When having children is especially important. I decide what's the best time for me. (10 = Always; 1 = Never)

1 2 3 4 5 6 7 8 9 10

5. Home should be managed carefully. Both my partner and I have the same authority in our home. (10 = Always; 1 = Never)

1 2 3 4 5 6 7 8 9 10

6. Happiness is one of my main goals. Improving my life is paramount. (10 = Always; 1 = Never)

1 2 3 4 5 6 7 8 9 10

7. I can see my life in many ways. I choose which perspective to have at each moment. (10 = Always; 1 = Never)

1 2 3 4 5 6 7 8 9 10

8. My path can be full of obstacles. I always find a way to get over them. (10 = Always; 1 = Never)

1 2 3 4 5 6 7 8 9 10

9. Unfortunate events can happen anytime. I always try to deal with them in the best practical way. (10 = Always; 1 = Never)

1 2 3 4 5 6 7 8 9 10

10. The attitude we take decides how we live our lives. I always try to take the best attitude to whatever may come. (10 = Always; 1 = Never)

1 2 3 4 5 6 7 8 9 10

Total score: _____

Define score:

0-29 = You don't manage your life at all.

30-59 = Sometimes you get to manage your life. However, it is not enough.

60-79 = You manage many aspects of your life. Keep improving!

80-100 = You not only manage your own life, but you are also your own hero.

Lesson #2

Lesson #2: We must rest. Not everything has to be work.

The Lesson Explained

Having and keeping a job is essential for us to consider ourselves as independent people. The time we devote to our work is of supreme importance, as this can determine the success we will have in the workplace. The author emphasizes several times that we must manage our lives in a way that we can be happy and productive, because that way we can feel self-realized. When it comes to work, many people try to be excessively productive, this leads them to work very excessive hours of work which exhaust them greatly. This can happen for many, many reasons, but the long-term consequences are profoundly serious. Therefore, it is necessary that people know how to identify when they are exceeding with their work so that they can establish a better work rhythm in their lives.

The author says that she herself was an overworked person. Because she worked long hours on a daily basis, stopping work caused her anxiety, so she always had to maintain a very demanding work routine. After a while, she began to realize that it was not good for her health or her life in general. Therefore, she had to take control and force herself to slow down the work rhythm of her life, as it was too intense.

To do this, she had to re-establish her own routine. This was because she had previously spent too many hours at work, so she didn't give herself the time to rest, think, relax, or just "do nothing." After setting herself up for more time for her own life, more time for herself, she began to feel a lot of anxiety, which was trying to force her to go back to her old routine in which she worked excessively. However, instead of succumbing to such anxiety she decided to support herself, sit down, have a glass of wine, and simply relax. With this, she realized that the world wouldn't stop spinning if she slowed down her work, if she spent more time on her personal life.

Application Exercise

Dedicating time to our work is important. However, we must also give ourselves time to relax and rest. Describe a situation in which you have decided to stop working because you want to give yourself more time.

Write Down Situation:

_____

_____

_____

_____

_____

What was your life like before that change?

_____

_____

_____

What made you make that change?

How did that change your life?

What did you decide to do with the time you gave yourself?

What do you think would have happened if you hadn't made that change in your life?

When you're done with the exercise: At the end of the exercise you will know more about the importance of having a balance in your life. Remember that you should always give yourself time to relax, think, or just do nothing.

Lesson #3

Lesson #3: In judging, we deny ourselves the right to see another person more deeply.

The Lesson Explained

Jealousy can lead us to look at life in an incredibly sad and pitiful way. Because we usually never admit that we are jealous of a certain person, we often try to hide it so that no one will notice what we are really feeling. However, this far from being good for our lives, makes us people who are only focused on the lives of others, so we downplay many things in our own lives.

On the other hand, besides being jealous, people are often extremely competitive, which leads us to only see other people as opponents or as possible opponents to whom we must then win and overcome; that is, prove that we are better than them. This means that we cannot establish relationships with other people in a deeper and more trusting way, since we will always try to look for negative things from these people in some way, as we would consider them our competitors. Among all the reasons why we can get to do this is because, whether we deny it or not, we are jealous of them.

When we are competitive or constantly jealous of people we often begin to judge other people in a very ignorant way. Because of how we choose to see other people, we can only see the surface of them, as we refuse to see beyond ourselves because we are being judgmental. The author explains to her readers that many times judging takes us away from relating to others in a closer and deeper way. Therefore, we cannot make more real and intense connections with other people because of the assumptions we make about them. These assumptions are based on what we see on the surface, so we get stuck there, unable to move forward or create stronger ties with those people. Because of this, the author helps us realize how we harm ourselves every time we try to bring others down.

Application Exercise

Judging other people only shows how much jealousy we are of them. Describe a situation in which you were jealous of someone and write down what you thought, assumed, and said.

Write Down Situation:

_____

_____

_____

_____

_____

Write down what I thought :

_____

_____

_____

Write down what I assumed:

_____

_____

_____

_____

Write down what I wished:

_____

_____

_____

_____

Write down what I said:

_____

_____

_____

_____

Write down what I did:

_____

_____

When you're done with the exercise: At the end of the exercise, you will be more aware of how harmful jealousy and judgment can be in your life. Remember that if you judge people without knowing anything about them, you can never create strong and lasting friendships.

Lesson #4

Lesson #4: We choose to be the person we believe we are.

The Lesson Explained

Throughout our lives we are progressively learning from our mistakes, since not only in one, but in several aspects of our lives we can make mistakes that we will have to fix so that our life can function properly. In addition to the mistakes we have made and may make, obstacles and problems can also arise in various aspects of our lives. Some of the most common problems in our lives are those that make our relationship with our partner difficult. Because that person is the one we choose to spend the rest of our lives with, many problems can arise for many reasons. Whether from an external problem or a problem between the relationship as such, these problems can have profound consequences in the future or can be a fantastic way to improve the marriage if they are viewed with the right attitude.

The author offers her readers a series of recommendations and suggestions to address these problems in the best practical way so that we can not only learn from them but avoid their recurrence in the future. She also recounts her own experiences with her partner and how they had to face many problems at the beginning of their relationship, which is very helpful for people who may be going through similar problems, as they will feel identified and will know that they are not the only ones who have gone through what they are going through.

Hollis emphasizes that problems as such are not the key point of what may happen because of them, the key point is our attitude and our decisions about them. Every day, problems of all kinds can appear, whether in our relationship, in our work, in our home, or even within ourselves, so we should not let those problems control us, but rather become much better versions of ourselves every time we overcome those problems. Therefore, it is not the problems that shape us, it is us. We choose how we act, we choose who we want to be with, we choose who we want to be.

Application Exercise

Many problems can arise in our lives. The true outcome of these problems will be determined by how we choose to address them. Below are a series of steps that will help you learn from the problems you have had or may have. (Choose one problem at a time)

Step one: Think about how that problem started.

_____

_____

_____

_____

Step two: Determine what changes that problem made to your life

_____

_____

Step three: Determine what you had to do to solve that problem.

_____

_____

_____

_____

_____

Step four: You already have the knowledge to solve these kinds of problems. Now think, what would you do if a problem like that came up again.

_____

_____

_____

_____

_____

Step five: Finally, determine the measures you could take to prevent this problem from recurring. Even though you know you can solve it, it is always better to have as few problems as possible.

_____

_____

Lesson #5

Lesson #5: The care we give to our own bodies says a lot about us.

The Lesson Explained

The importance of body image can be based on many aspects that often vary from person to person. Some people think this isn't important, so for them, body image is something we shouldn't worry about, because for them, inner beauty says everything about us, while body image says nothing. On the other hand, other people think just the opposite. For those people, body image is everything, not only because they judge other people according to their weight, appearance, or defects, but also because they judge themselves and force themselves to become people with a "perfect" body image. They do this because they do not want to be like the other people they judge, but they want to turn their body into one that cannot be judged because it would have no defects.

These people often develop eating disorders or other long-term problems that make their lives exceedingly difficult without them realizing it many times over. Hollis says she was like that. For a long time, she had had problems with her body image because she didn't allow herself to have any defects. For her, having a little extra weight or any other "defect" was something she could not tolerate. In short, for her, her weight defined her, her weight defined people. This perspective on body image led her to develop eating problems and make it much more difficult to deal with other problems such as facial paralysis.

Because of this, she says that weight is not what defines us. However, our body image says a lot about us, not because of our defects, height, or appearance, but because of the appreciation and care we give to it. She thinks that true beauty is not found in a body that claims to be perfect by maintaining the right weight or hiding all its defects, but in one that is cared and taken into consideration by the person.

Application Exercise

Our body image says a lot about us, as it reflects how much care we take of our body. However, true beauty is not found in a "perfect body," but in a well-cared for body. Think of a time in your life when you believed that having the ideal weight was everything and describe what you felt, thought, and did when you felt that your weight was not the right one.

Write Down Situation:

_____

_____

_____

_____

_____

Write down what I felt:

_____

_____

_____

Write down what I thought:

Write down what I assumed:

Write down what I did:

Write down what I ate:

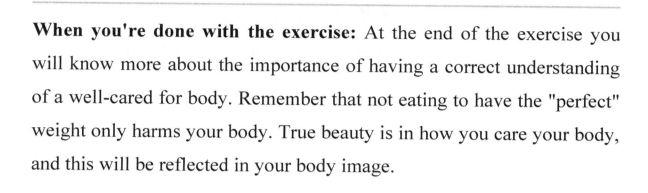

When you're done with the exercise: At the end of the exercise you will know more about the importance of having a correct understanding of a well-cared for body. Remember that not eating to have the "perfect" weight only harms your body. True beauty is in how you care your body, and this will be reflected in your body image.

Attention: Bonus Download

Thank you for your purchase of Max Help Workbooks

Get Free Workbooks with <u>**Any Purchase**</u> *of* Max Help Workbooks

Every purchase comes with a FREE download!

Get it Now

or Click Here.

Lesson #6

Lesson #6: We must not abandon our dreams. We must create for ourselves the life we dream of having.

The Lesson Explained

The life we have is not always the life we want. This can be very traumatic, exceedingly difficult, awfully hard. However, the fact that our life may at some point be that way does not mean that we must give up on our dreams and let ourselves be carried away by the misfortunes that may befall us. Hollis recounts about her childhood, and how things happened that made it very traumatic and difficult. She describes how she was affected by the problems that several members of her family had. On one hand, her mother was a person who stayed in bed for weeks, while on the other hand, her own older brother committed suicide. All of this made Hollis' early life very chaotic, extremely hard, hard enough that she wanted to stay stuck in the trauma and never get over it.

Because of this, she emphasizes that regardless of what may happen in our lives, it is in our own hands whether we move forward or get stuck. She says that we all have the power not only to recover from the damage we have suffered for one reason or another, but also to improve our lives and make it into what we have always wanted. Therefore, if we are not happy with the life we have, it is only in our power to improve it, and for that, we have to follow our dreams, as they show us the way to our own happiness.

Hollis says that we should not consider our dreams as unimportant goals to be achieved or as silly things. On the contrary, we must embrace them and do all we can to fulfil them. We should not leave it up to anyone to decide what is best for us or to affect what we think about our dreams. Nor should we let those opinions decide what we are worth, but we should believe in our dreams and let ourselves be guided by them, because only they will lead us to the life we have always wanted to have.

Application Exercise

Our dreams must be the ones that guide us in our lives. These are the ones that will truly create the path we must follow. Below are a series of steps that will help you begin to follow your dreams and create the life you really want.

Step one: Think about what your life would be like in the future if you could fulfill all your dreams.

_____

_____

_____

_____

Step two: Think about what it would feel like to just know that you have achieved your dreams, that you have fulfilled your goals, and that you have the life you wanted.

_____

Step three: Now determine what possible obstacles you had to overcome in order to get there.

_____

_____

_____

_____

Step four: Determine what you had to achieve or what you had to get based on your current situation up to the desired situation.

_____

_____

_____

_____

Step five: With this, you already have a path to follow, since this path is based on your dream, on what you want to do. Now you know what you must accomplish and/or get and the problems that are likely to come your way. Take the first step and do not stop.

_____

_____

_____

Lesson #7

Lesson #7: Our dreams aren't something someone else can manage. We must be our own bosses.

The Lesson Explained

Much of what we do defines who we will be. Depending on how we act and with what perspective we see the world, we can become extraordinarily successful and fulfill all our dreams or simply abandon them. Hollis recounts her own story of her path to be the successful woman she is today. We can notice that in the beginning, she only had her ideas, dreams, and aspirations. By letting them guide her, she was able to gather the courage to follow the path that showed her her dreams and be a remarkably successful person.

She relates that even before she was eighteen years old, she left home to fulfill her dreams. She moved to Los Angeles to have more opportunities to put her ideas into action. She explains that the reason she has worked so hard and continues to do so is because she really loves her job. Working, for her, is a joy, it's something she's grateful for. For that reason, she has been able to achieve so much in so little time. At the age of twenty-one, Hollis had some agreements in Hollywood and was even in charge of a business where events were planned. Later in 2008, she was named one of the 30 most successful entrepreneurs under 30 by INC Magazine.

She explains that our dreams cannot be managed by anyone but us. We are the only ones who can make them come true, because only we know what we really want. She says she became successful because she realized that no one can tell her how big her dreams are, because she never took no for an answer, because she became her own boss. Currently, Hollis is the CEO of her own company, Chic Media. This website is focused on lifestyle topics and has approximately two million readers annually. In addition, through her business, Hollis has established contracts with companies such as JCPenney, Covergirl, Walmart, among others.

Application Exercise

In order to fulfill our dreams, we must take control of our lives and our decisions, for this, we must be our own bosses. Describe a situation in which you have chosen to be the boss of your own business.

Write Down Situation:

_____

_____

_____

_____

Why did 5you decide to be the boss of your own business?

_____

_____

How did it feel to be your own boss?

What was your life like before you decided to be your own boss?

What do you think would have happened if you hadn't been your own boss?

How did this help fulfill your dreams?

_____

_____

_____

_____

When you're done with the exercise: At the end of the exercise you will be more aware of the importance of managing your dreams with your own hands. To do this, we have to be our own bosses, that is, the owners of our future.

Lesson #8

Lesson #8: God gives us the tools. We choose how to use them.

The Lesson Explained

God gives us support, strength, and love so that we can live our lives in a way that we can laugh, enjoy, surpass ourselves, and move forward despite the problems that may arise. In addition, so that we can fulfill our dreams, God gives us the necessary tools so that we can overcome the obstacles that may appear in our path. God gives us the tools not only to live our lives in a way that we can feel satisfied and fulfilled, but also to be better people every day. Everything depends on our own decisions, on how we use the tools and support that God gives us, because if we use them correctly, they can take us where we want to go, they can help us become the person we want to be.

Hollis explains that for as long as she can remember, she has believed in God's presence and that God is in control of her life. She believes wholeheartedly that God is the one who guides her, who supports her, who gives her strength and love. She says that many times this may not be easy, since life can be so tough that it makes us doubt about our own beliefs and our own faith. However, she does believe that God has a plan for her life.

She explains that she began to believe in God in the beginning because she is the daughter of the preacher of her small hometown. Therefore, she grew up being a Christian and learning many of the teachings of this religion. She learned that God is in control and she also learned to believe in this from the depth of her heart, from the depth of her bones. However, Hollis also believes that even if God gives us the tools—which can be gifts, opportunities, talents, among others—that doesn't mean we should waste them simply because we believe we've accomplished enough and are already good enough. Hollis believes that God loves us all unconditionally, and that we should use the tools he gives us in the best way we can.

Application Exercise

God guides us, supports us, and gives us strength. This, together with the tools he gives us, allows us to fulfill our dreams and live the life we want. Describe a situation in which you noticed that God gave you the tools you needed to improve and write down what you felt, thought, and did.

Write Down Situation:

_____

_____

_____

_____

Write down what I felt:

_____

Write down what I thought:

Write down what I assumed:

Write down what I did:

Write down how I improved:

_____

_____

_____

_____

When you're done with the exercise: At the end of the exercise, you will be more aware that God is in control of our lives and that He will always give us what we need to be better. Remember that even though God gives us the tools, we are the ones who decide how to use them, so we must always use them in the best possible way.

Bonus Application Worksheet

OUR FREE GIFT TO YOU!

Bonus Worksheet

Quiz Questions

1. We must find a way to be happy. We must be our own
   _____.

2. Trying to be _____ doesn't make us selfish. Nor does it
   take us away from our beliefs or religion.

3. For some people, stopping work can cause _____. These
   people should force themselves to relax and simply rest.

4. Through _____ and jealousy, we can keep many people
   away. In addition, we also forbid ourselves to have deeper and more
   intense relationships.

5. Many problems can arise in our lives. However, _____
   are the ones who determine how these problems affect us, we choose
   who we are.

6. Body _____ can tell a lot about us. Not because of our weight or appearance, but because of the care we take of our bodies.

7. Our _____ show us the path we must follow. Therefore, we must never abandon them.

8. Only we can manage our own dreams. We must be our own _____.

9. _____ gives us the tools. We choose how to use them.

10. Rachel Hollis is CEO of her own company. This company is called Chic Media. (T/F)

11. Rachel Hollis is a Catholic. She's the daughter of the preacher in her hometown. (T/F)

12. Rachel Hollis has contracted with several companies through her business. Some of them are: JCPenney, Walmart, Target, among others. (T/F)

Quiz Answer

1. Heroes

2. Happy

3. Anxiety

4. Judgment

5. We

6. Image

7. Dreams

8. Bosses

9. God

10. True. Rachel Hollis is CEO of her own company. This company is called Chic Media.

11. False. Rachel Hollis is a Christian. She's the daughter of the preacher in her hometown.

12. True. Rachel Hollis has contracted with several companies through her business. Some of them are: JCPenney, Walmart, Target, among others.

Attention: Bonus Download

Thank you for your purchase of Max Help Workbooks

Get Free Workbooks with **_Any Purchase_** *of* Max Help Workbooks

Every purchase comes with a FREE download!

Get it Now

or Click Here.

CPSIA information can be obtained
at www.ICGtesting.com
Printed in the USA
BVHW011816141219
566691BV00011B/377/P